Sandburg Middle School

VIOLIN
80VN

All for STRINGS
COMPREHENSIVE STRING METHOD ▪ BOOK 3
by Gerald E. Anderson and Robert S. Frost

D1312016

Dear String Student:

Welcome to **ALL FOR STRINGS, Book 3!**

By now, you have discovered that careful study and regular practice have brought you the joy and satisfaction of playing beautiful music.

The new playing technics and musical concepts found in **ALL FOR STRINGS, Book 3** will help you to continue your progress as a string player and musician.

We hope that **ALL FOR STRINGS, Book 3** will help make the road to your musical goals more enjoyable.

Best wishes!

Gerald E. Anderson
Robert S. Frost

ALL FOR STRINGS, Book 3 is published for the following instruments:
Violin   Viola   Cello   String Bass

Piano Accompaniment
   A separate book containing 89 piano accompaniments is recommended to students for home use, private instruction and ensemble practice.

ISBN 0-8497-3304-9

KJOS NEIL A. KJOS MUSIC COMPANY ▪ SAN DIEGO, CALIFORNIA

TUNING

1. TUNE YOUR INSTRUMENT

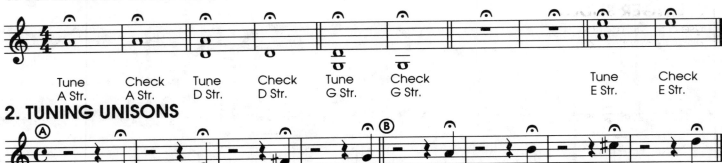

| Tune A Str. | Check A Str. | Tune D Str. | Check D Str. | Tune G Str. | Check G Str. | | Tune E Str. | Check E Str. |

2. TUNING UNISONS

THEORY GAME

3. TUNING CHORDS (Root position)

★ What does "simile" mean? _____

4. TUNING CHORDS (Inversions)

5. TUNING CHORD PROGRESSIONS

6. A MIGHTY FORTRESS

Luther

VIBRATO

DEVELOP FINGER STRENGTH

7. FINGER SLIDES

Use a finger motion only. Move the sliding finger from a curved position to a straight position and back to a curved position. Keep the finger(s) below the sliding finger down in one location.

★ Be sure you have a good left hand position.

DEVELOP CORRECT VIBRATO MOTION

8. WAVE GOOD-BYE

   a. Without your instrument, place your left arm in playing position with the palm of your left hand facing you.
   b. Wave good-bye to yourself. Wave only your hand keeping your arm still. The wave should be from the wrist. This is the basic vibrato motion.

9. POLISHING THE STRING

With your instrument only (no bow), play Exercises a. and b. using the rhythms below in both of the following positions:

      • Regular playing position with the end of the scroll against the wall.
      • Regular playing position.

   a. Place your 2nd finger lightly on the A string. Move your hand and thumb back and forth with a vibrato motion with your 2nd finger lightly sliding on the string as if polishing the string. Do this with each of your fingers. See Diagram 1.

   b. Place your thumb in one place (regular playing position) against the neck. Lightly slide each finger back and forth with a vibrato motion as you did in exercise 9a. Do not slide the thumb. See Diagram 2.

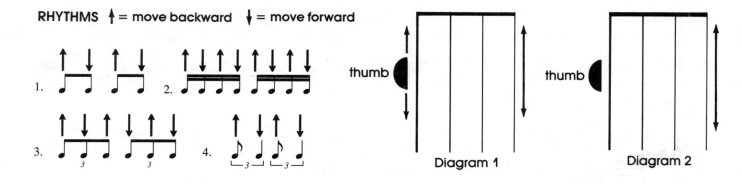

RHYTHMS ↑ = move backward ↓ = move forward

PLAY WITH VIBRATO

THEORY GAME

10. TETRACHORD SCALES

Play these tetrachord scales with a smooth and relaxed vibrato on each note. Rest when your hand gets tired.

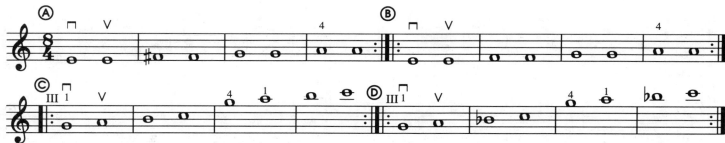

★ How many beats in a measure does $\frac{8}{4}$ time have? _____

4

11. C MAJOR

★ Apply the following bowings to lines 11 and 12. Also apply these bowings to lines 15, 16, 19, and 20.

12. C MAJOR REVIEW

Wohlfahrt Op. 45, no. 2

13. WELCOME TO ALL

Schubert-Round

Moderato

★ Begin your pick-up note in the middle of the bow.

14. "NEW WORLD" SYMPHONY-THEME

Dvořák

Largo*

D. C. al Fine

★ Play this piece using vibrato.
* Refer to page 18 for the tempo/dynamic glossary.

15. F MAJOR

★ Apply the following bowings to lines 15 and 16. Also apply these bowings to lines 11, 12, 19, and 20.

16. F MAJOR REVIEW

Wohlfahrt Op. 54, no. 1

★ Play all 4th fingers as marked to strengthen your hand position.

17. THE BRITISH GRENADIERS

Schumann

* Refer to page 18 for the tempo/dynamic glossary.

18. THREE PIRATES

English Sea Chantey

6

19. D MAJOR

★ Apply the following bowings to lines 19 and 20. Also apply these bowings to lines 11, 12, 15, and 16.

   a.   b.   c.   d.

20. D MAJOR REVIEW

Werner Op. 12

THEORY GAME

21. ALL THROUGH THE NIGHT

Welsh Folk Song

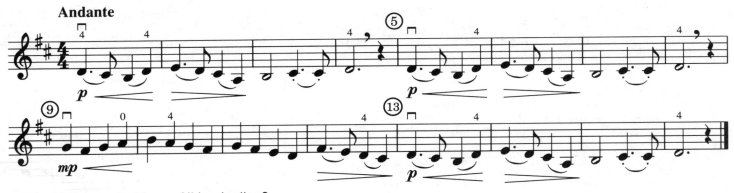

Andante

★ What is the musical form of this selection? _____

22. A CAPITAL SHIP

American Folk Song

Vivace*

* Refer to page 18 for the tempo/dynamic glossary.

23. THE IRISH WASHERWOMAN

Traditional

★ Also play this piece without slurs, as shown:

24. JIG

Irish Folk Song

★ Observe accents and staccato marks in lines 24 and 25.

25. MAZURKA

Wohlfahrt Op. 38, no. 62

NEW IDEA

THEORY GAME

DOTTED EIGHTH AND SIXTEENTH NOTES

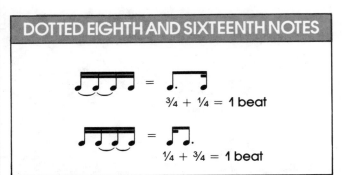

$\frac{3}{4} + \frac{1}{4} = 1$ beat

$\frac{1}{4} + \frac{3}{4} = 1$ beat

Counting		1 e & a	2 e & a
Alternate Counting			

26. RHYTHM TRAINER

★ 1. Write in the counting. 2. Clap and count each line. 3. Play arco or pizzicato.
   4. Practice each rhythm/bowing on the descending scale.

27. TECHNIC TRAINER

28. BATTLE HYMN OF THE REPUBLIC

Steffe

Moderato

mp

cresc.

f

rit.

THEORY GAME

★ Begin your pick-up note in the middle of the bow.   What does "rit." mean? _____

29. THE MARRIAGE OF FIGARO — ARIA

Mozart

Allegro

30. TECHNIC TRAINER

★ Play this exercise with the following bowings:

a.   b.   c.   d.

31. LA DONNA E MOBILE

Verdi

Allegro

32. RHYTHM TEASER

★ 1. Write in the counting.   2. Clap and count.   3. Play arco or pizzicato.

33. COLONIAL HYMN

Billings-Round

Lento*

★ Play this piece using vibrato.

* Refer to page 18 for the tempo/dynamic glossary.

NEW IDEA

TIME SIGNATURE	$\frac{3}{8}$ = 3 beats in each measure

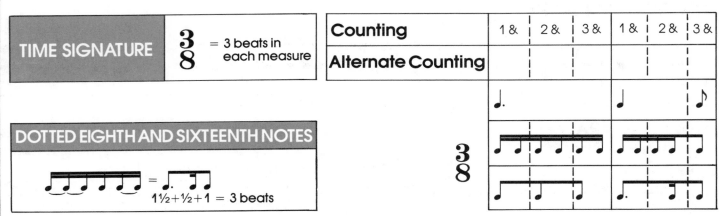

Counting	1 &	2 &	3 &	1 &	2 &	3 &
Alternate Counting						

DOTTED EIGHTH AND SIXTEENTH NOTES

1½ + ½ + 1 = 3 beats

THEORY GAME

34. RHYTHM TRAINER

★ 1. Write in the counting. 2. Clap and count each line. 3. Play arco or pizzicato.
  4. Practice each bowing/rhythm on the descending scale.

35. RHYTHMIC WALTZ

Wohlfahrt Op. 38, no. 66

Moderato

Melody

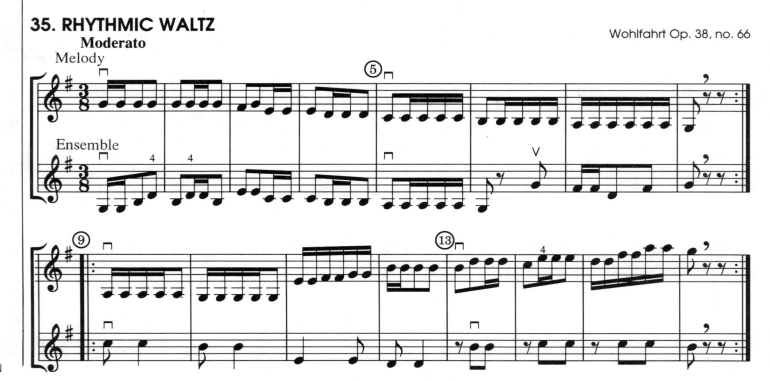

36. RHYTHM TEASER

THEORY GAME

★ 1. Write in the counting. 2. Clap and count. 3. Play arco or pizzicato.

37. SCHEHERAZADE

Rimsky-Korsakov

Allegro moderato

★ Use smooth bow changes.

38. TECHNIC TRAINER

★ Play this exercise with the following bowings:

a.   b.   c.   d.   e.   f.

39. GREENSLEEVES

Old English Air

Moderato

rit.

40. SANTA LUCIA

Neapolitan Boat Song

Andante

rit.

NEW IDEA

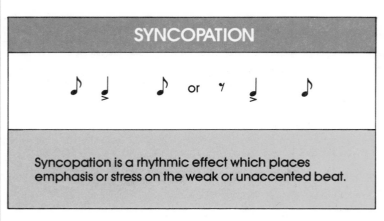

SYNCOPATION

Syncopation is a rhythmic effect which places emphasis or stress on the weak or unaccented beat.

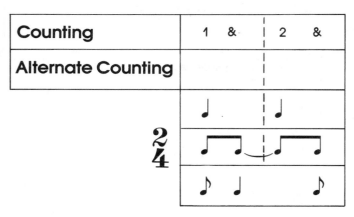

Counting	1	&	2	&
Alternate Counting				

THEORY GAME

41. RHYTHM TRAINER

★ 1. Write in the counting. 2. Clap and count each line. 3. Play arco or pizzicato.
4. Practice each rhythm/bowing on the descending scale.

42. THE RIDDLE

Kentucky Folk Tune

43. POLKA

Slovakian Folk Song

* Refer to page 18 for the tempo/dynamic glossary.

44. GO DOWN MOSES

Spiritual

Andante

★ Play this piece using vibrato.

45. RHYTHM TEASER

★ 1. Write in the counting. 2. Clap and count. 3. Play arco or pizzicato.

46. CARRY ME BACK TO OLD VIRGINNY

Bland

Moderato

★ Play this piece in the middle of the bow. Save bow on the ♩. How many measures use syncopation? _____

47. DIXIE

Emmett

Allegro

NEW IDEA

KEY SIGNATURE		This is the key signature for Eb Major. When you see this key signature, play all the B's as Bb, all the E's as Eb, and all the A's as Ab.

48. Eb MAJOR SCALE AND BROKEN THIRDS

★ Refer to pages 46, 47, and the inside back cover for other bowing and scale possibilities.

49. Eb MAJOR TRAINER

★ Play this exercise with the following bowings:

a.   b.   c.   d.

50. CRUSADER'S HYMN

German Air

Moderato

Melody

Ensemble

★ Play this piece using vibrato.

51. AUSTRIAN HYMN

Haydn

52. LAZY SAMMY

Hebrew-Round

53. MY OLD KENTUCKY HOME

Foster

★ Begin your pick-up note close to the frog of the bow.
* Refer to page 18 for the tempo/dynamic glossary.

54. WOODEN SHOE DANCE

Belgian Folk Song

★ *2x rit.* tells you to ritard. the second time through the piece.

KEY SIGNATURE  This is the key signature for c minor. It is the same key signature as E♭ Major because c minor is the relative minor key.

55. C MINOR SCALES AND ARPEGGIOS

★ Refer to pages 46, 47, and the inside back cover for other bowing and scale possibilities.

56. C MINOR TRAINER

★ Play this exercise with the following bowings:

a.   b.   c.   d.

57. RISE UP O FLAME

Praetorius-Round

58. FARANDOLE

Bizet

D. C. al Fine

NEW IDEA

| KEY SIGNATURE | | This is the key signature for E Major. When you see this key signature, play all the F's as F♯, all the C's as C♯, all the G's as G♯, and all the D's as D♯. |

59. E MAJOR SCALE AND BROKEN THIRDS

★ Refer to pages 46, 47, and the inside back cover for other bowing and scale possibilities.

60. E MAJOR TRAINER

★ Play this exercise with the following bowings:

a. b. c. d.

61. IN THE GLOAMING

Harrison

62. LOVELY MONTH OF MAY

Schubert-Round

NEW IDEA

| SFORZANDO | sfz | Sforzando is a strong accent on a particular note or chord. |

63. THE BARTERED BRIDE

Smetana

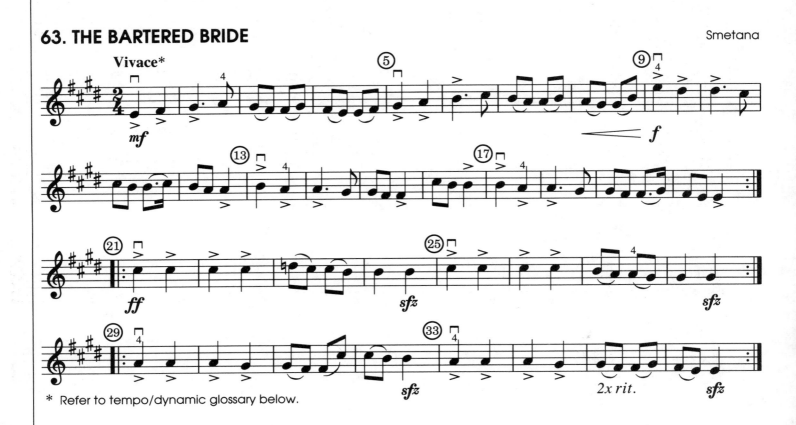

Vivace*

* Refer to tempo/dynamic glossary below.

NEW IDEA

| TEMPOS | The Italian terms listed below represent the most common tempo and dynamic markings used in classical music. | DYNAMICS |

Presto	very fast			
Vivace	brisk and animated	$f\!f$	Fortissimo	very loud
Allegro	quick and lively	f	Forte	loud
Moderato	moderate speed	mf	Mezzo forte	moderately loud
Andante	moderately slow	mp	Mezzo piano	moderately soft
Lento	slow, between Adagio and Andante	p	Piano	soft
Adagio	slow and leisurely, not as slow as Largo	pp	Pianissimo	very soft
Largo	very slow and broad	cresc.	Crescendo	increasing in loudness
a tempo	in the original speed	dim.	Diminuendo	diminishing in loudness
rit.	Ritard. gradually slow the speed			

DYNAMIC CHART

pp p mp mf f $f\!f$ f mf mp p pp

NEW IDEA

NEW NOTES

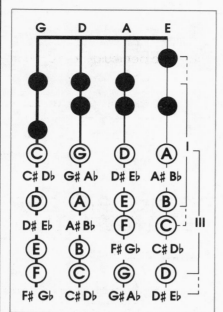

64. THIRD POSITION TRAINER FOR VIOLINS AND VIOLAS

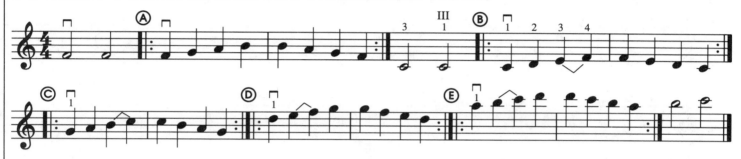

65. C MAJOR SCALE, BROKEN THIRDS AND ARPEGGIOS

66. MARINES' HYMN

Offenbach

Allegro

80VN

67. TECHNIC TRAINER

★ Play this exercise with the following bowings:

a. b. c. d.

68. ANNIE LAURIE

Scottish Folk Song

★ Play this piece using vibrato.

69. G MAJOR SCALE, BROKEN THIRDS AND ARPEGGIOS

70. RONDEAU

Mouret

71. THE MINSTREL BOY

Irish Folk Song

★ Circle the notes played with the 1st finger.

72. TECHNIC TRAINER

73. D MAJOR SCALE, BROKEN THIRDS AND ARPEGGIOS

74. JOY TO THE WORLD

Handel

Allegro moderato

75. TECHNIC TRAINER

★ Work for smooth string crossings.

76. BOHEMIAN FOLK SONG

Traditional

77. F MAJOR SCALE, BROKEN THIRDS AND ARPEGGIOS

78. BARBARA ALLEN

English Folk Song

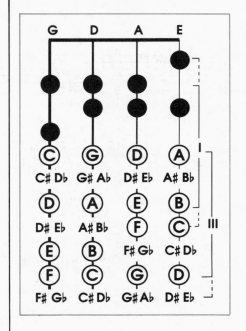

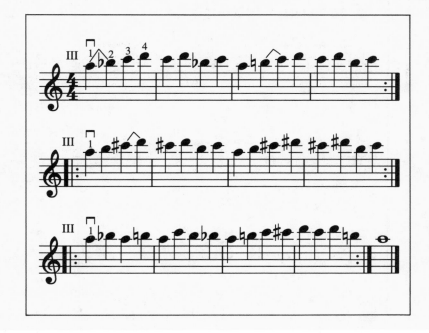

79. THIRD POSITION TRAINER FOR CELLOS

80. ORIGINAL FOLK DANCE

Anderson

Allegro moderato

★ Circle the notes played with the 2nd finger.

81. ETUDE FOR CELLO

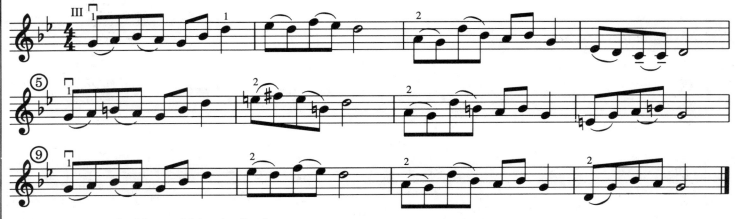

★ What is the musical form of this selection? _____

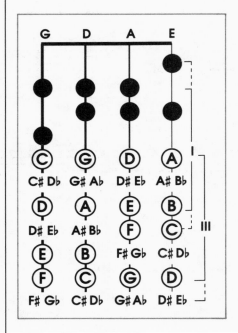

82. FOURTH POSITION TRAINER FOR CELLOS

83. MELODIC ETUDE IN A MINOR

Déak Vol. 1, no. 49

FROM: MODERN METHOD FOR THE VIOLONCELLO – Vol. I
© 1929 Elkan-Vogel, Inc.
Reprinted By Permission Of The Publisher

THEORY
GAME

84. LAMENT

Anderson

Lento

★ What does "Lento" mean? _____

D. C. al Fine

85. TECHNIC TRAINER

★ Play this exercise with the following bowings:

a. b. c. d. e.

86. ANDANTINO

Werner Op. 12, no. 10a

★ Circle the notes played with the 3rd finger.

87. MELODIC ETUDE IN F MAJOR

Kummer

88. BARCAROLLE

Offenbach

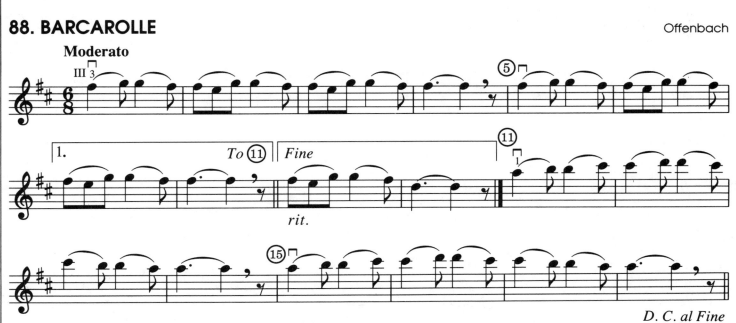

★ Play this piece using vibrato. Write in your own dynamics for this piece. Be sure to use crescendos and diminuendos.

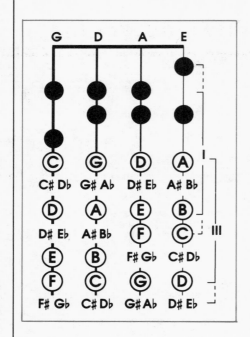

89. E MAJOR SCALE

90. THE OLD WOMAN AND THE PEDDLER

English Folk Song

91. F MAJOR SCALE

92. ETUDE FOR BASS

SHIFTING TO THE SAME FINGER – CLASS 1 SHIFT (Ascending)

First (I) Position to Third (III) Position

SHIFTING INSTRUCTIONS

1. Move your hand, thumb, fingers, and forearm together.
2. Lead with your wrist in the direction of the shift.
3. Slightly release the pressure of the sliding finger during the shift.
4. Keep the sliding finger in contact with the string during the shift.
5. Keep your hand, thumb, and forearm relaxed.
6. Slow down the bow speed and lighten the bow pressure during the shift.

EXERCISE INSTRUCTIONS

1. Play the first measure of each exercise to establish intonation.
2. Play the second measure of each exercise to practice the shift.
3. Play each exercise also slurring 2 notes: ♩ ♩ ♩ ♩
4. These exercises should NOT be practiced all at one time. Select and practice a few exercises each day. Especially practice shifts encountered in your repertoire.
5. Apply the following key signatures to each section in order to practice the various finger spacings.

I. FIRST FINGER SHIFTS

II. SECOND FINGER SHIFTS

III. THIRD FINGER SHIFTS

IV. FOURTH FINGER SHIFTS

28

SHIFTING TO THE SAME FINGER – CLASS 1 SHIFT (Ascending)

NEW IDEA

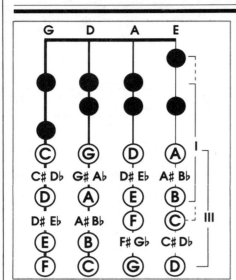

First (I) Position to Third (III) Position

SHIFTING INSTRUCTIONS

1. Move your hand, thumb, fingers, and forearm together.
2. Lead with your wrist in the direction of the shift.
3. Slightly release the pressure of the sliding finger during the shift.
4. Keep the sliding finger in contact with the string during the shift.
5. Keep your hand, thumb, and forearm relaxed.
6. Slow down the bow speed and lighten the bow pressure during the shift.

93. SHIFTING TRAINER

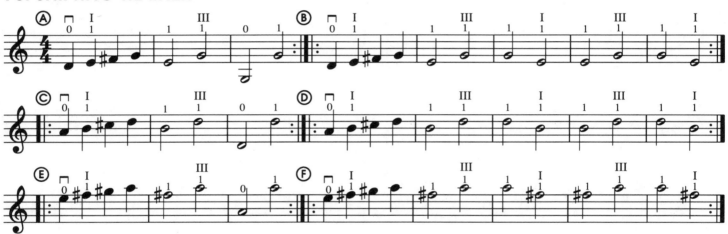

94. MARINES' HYMN

Offenbach

95. NIFTY SHIFTER

Anderson

★ Keep the sliding finger in contact with the string during the shift.

96. SHIFTING TRAINER

97. POLLY WOLLY DOODLE

American Folk Song

★ Play this piece with your best tone at all dynamic levels. What does "Presto" mean? _____

98. SHIFTING ETUDE NO. 1

Wohlfahrt Op. 74, no. 36

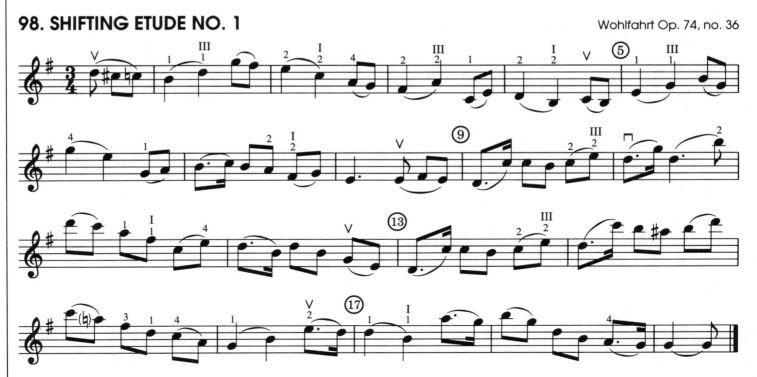

★ Keep the sliding finger in contact with the string during the shift.

99. AIR

Frost

100. SHIFTING TRAINER

101. RUSSIAN FOLK SONG

Traditional

102. SHIFTING ETUDE NO. 2

Wohlfahrt Op. 45, no. 39

★ Keep the sliding finger in contact with the string during the shift.

103. CHORALE PRELUDE

Bach

Moderato

104. SHIFTING TRAINER

105. ALL FINGERS SHIFT

106. SONGS MY MOTHER TAUGHT ME

Dvořák

Andante

THEORY GAME

★ How many measures use syncopation? _____

107. ONE BY ONE

★ Keep your 1st finger in contact with the string during the shift.

SHIFTING TO A DIFFERENT FINGER – CLASS 2 SHIFT (Ascending)

Low Numbered Finger to a High Numbered Finger
First (I) Position to Third (III) Position

SHIFTING INSTRUCTIONS

1. Shift up or down with the finger last used in the old position. This finger becomes the shifting guide finger.
2. Place the new finger immediately upon reaching the new position.
3. Move your fingers, hand, and forearm in a relaxed motion during the shift.

EXERCISE INSTRUCTIONS

1. These exercises should NOT be practiced all at one time. Select and practice a few exercises each day. Especially practice the shifts encountered in your repertoire.
2. Apply the following key signatures in order to practice the various finger spacings.

I. E STRING

II. A STRING

NEW IDEA

SHIFTING TO A DIFFERENT FINGER – CLASS 2 SHIFT (Ascending)

Low Numbered Finger to a High Numbered Finger
First (I) Position to Third (III) Position

SHIFTING INSTRUCTIONS

1. Shift up or down with the finger last used in the old position. This finger becomes the shifting guide finger.
2. Place the new finger immediately upon reaching the new position.
3. Move your fingers, hand, and forearm in a relaxed motion during the shift.

108. SHIFTING TRAINER NO. 1

★ The descending shift is to the same finger.

109. SHIFTING TRAINER NO. 2

★ The descending shift is to a different finger.

110. SHIFTING ETUDE

Fine

★ Shift to the new position using the guide finger.

D. C. al Fine

111. THE LION TAMER

Frost

Allegro Moderato

112. TO A WILD ROSE
MacDowell

★ Play this piece using vibrato.

113. APRIL
Brahms

★ Play with your best tone.

114. MELODY*
Rubinstein

* This song is originally known as "Melody in F."

D. C. al Fine

115. SHIFTING SERENADE
Anderson

★ Shift to the new position using the guide finger.

D. C. al Fine

SHIFTING TO A DIFFERENT FINGER – CLASS 3 SHIFT (Ascending)

High Numbered Finger to a Low Numbered Finger
First (I) Position to Third (III) Position

SHIFTING INSTRUCTIONS

METHOD I
1. Shift up with the finger to be used in the new position. This finger becomes the shifting guide finger.
2. Move your fingers, hand, and forearm in a relaxed motion during the shift.

OR

METHOD II
1. Shift up with the finger last used in the old position. This finger becomes the shifting guide finger.
2. Place the new finger immediately upon reaching the new position.
3. Move your fingers, hand, and forearm in a relaxed motion during the shift.

EXERCISE INSTRUCTIONS

1. These exercises should NOT be practiced all at one time. Select and practice a few exercises each day.
   Especially practice the shifts encountered in your repertoire.
2. Apply the following key signatures in order to practice the various finger spacings.

METHOD I
E STRING

A STRING

METHOD II
E STRING

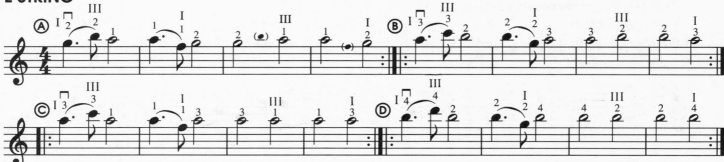

A STRING

NEW IDEA

SHIFTING TO A DIFFERENT FINGER – CLASS 3 SHIFT (Ascending)

High Numbered Finger to a Low Numbered Finger
First (I) Position to Third (III) Position

Two methods of shifting for the Class 3 shift are presented below in line 116. Your teacher will tell you which method to use.

SHIFTING INSTRUCTIONS

METHOD I
1. Shift with the finger to be used in the new position. This finger becomes the shifting guide finger.
2. Move your fingers, hand, and forearm in a relaxed motion during the shift.

OR

METHOD II
1. Shift up with the finger last used in the old position. This finger becomes the shifting guide finger.
2. Place the new finger immediately upon reaching the new position.
3. Move your fingers, hand, and forearm in a relaxed motion during the shift.

116. SHIFTING TRAINER

METHOD I

METHOD II

(Cello only I to IV Pos.)

METHOD I   **METHOD II**

117. SHIFTING ETUDE

★ Play this exercise with the following bowings:

118. BENEATH THY GUIDING HAND

Hatton

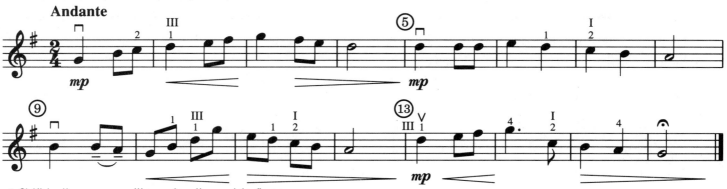

★ Shift to the new position using the guide finger.

119. HOME ON THE RANGE

Cowboy Song

★ Play this piece using vibrato.

120. CANON

Tallis

121. SWEET THE EVENING AIR OF MAY

Hungarian-Round

D. C. al Fine

NEW IDEA

SHIFTING FROM AN OPEN STRING TO A NEW POSITION
– CLASS 4 SHIFT

First (I) Position to Third (III) Position

SHIFTING INSTRUCTIONS

1. Shift to new position while playing the open string.
2. Move your fingers, hand, and forearm in a relaxed motion during the shift.
3. Review the Class 1 Shift if you are unsure of the distance your fingers, hand, and forearm should travel for this shift.

122. SHIFTING TRAINER

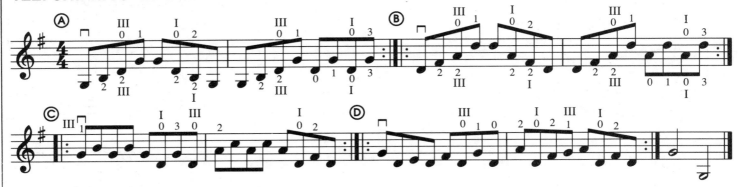

123. SHIFTING ETUDE

Wohlfahrt Op. 45, no. 36

124. FLOW GENTLY, SWEET AFTON

Scottish Folk Song

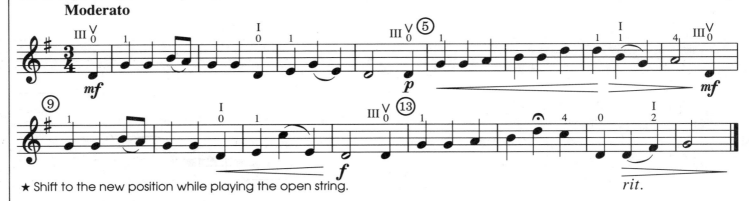

★ Shift to the new position while playing the open string.

125. SONG OF TRIUMPH

Slovakian Folk Song

SOLOS

126. MARCH
Bach

127. VIOLIN CONCERTO—THEME
Mendelssohn

128. MINUET IN G—TRIO
Beethoven

NEW IDEA

NEW NOTE

| HARMONIC |  G String | A natural harmonic is produced by touching the string lightly on the note shown. It is marked by a small o above the note. |

129. HARMONICS

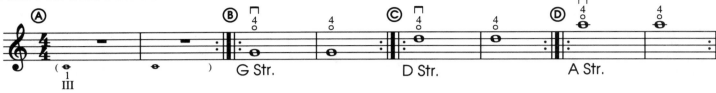

G Str.　　　D Str.　　　A Str.

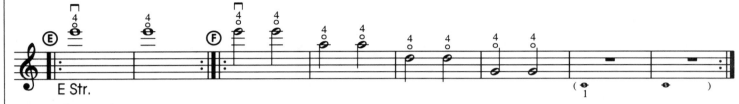

E Str.

130. TECHNIC TRAINER

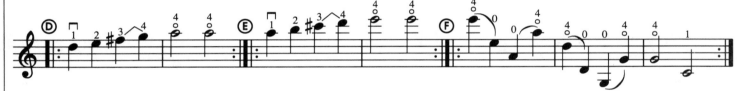

131. SOUTHERN ROSES

Strauss

Vivace

★ Play this piece using vibrato.

132. ALL THROUGH THE NIGHT

Welsh Folk Song

Andante

★ Touch the string lightly with the finger shown to produce a clear harmonic.

Page 41

133. TECHNIC TRAINER

134. HATIKVAH

Hebrew Song

135. TECHNIC TRAINER

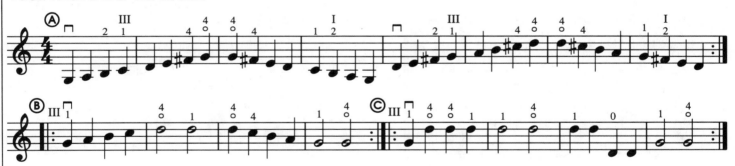

THEORY GAME

136. ENGLISH FOLK SONG

Traditional

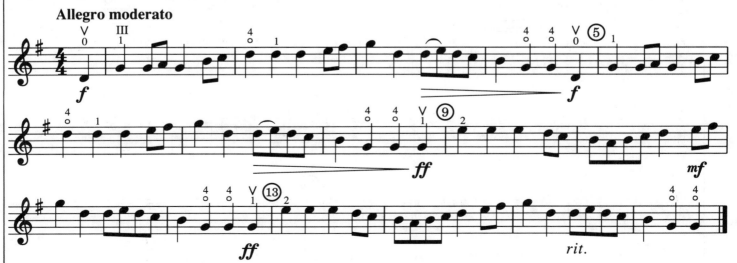

★ What is the musical form of this selection? _____   Circle the notes played with the 4th finger.

80VN

NEW IDEA

NEW NOTE

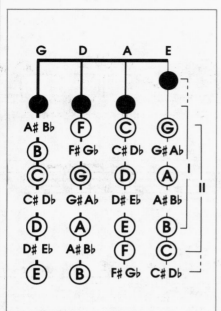

137. SECOND POSITION TRAINER FOR VIOLINS AND VIOLAS

138. F MAJOR SCALE, BROKEN THIRDS AND ARPEGGIOS

139. SICILIAN SONG

Traditional

THEORY GAME

★ Choose an appropriate tempo marking for this piece. Refer to page 18.

140. SIMPLE GIFTS

Shaker Melody

★ Circle the 1st finger notes that are played in 2nd position.

141. C MAJOR SCALE, BROKEN THIRDS AND ARPEGGIOS

142. ARKANSAS TRAVELER

American Folk Song

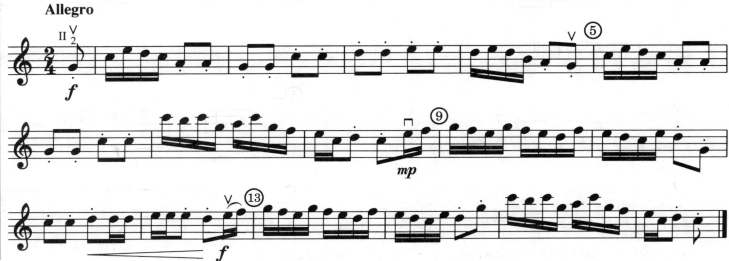

ETUDES

143. G MAJOR ETUDE

Lee

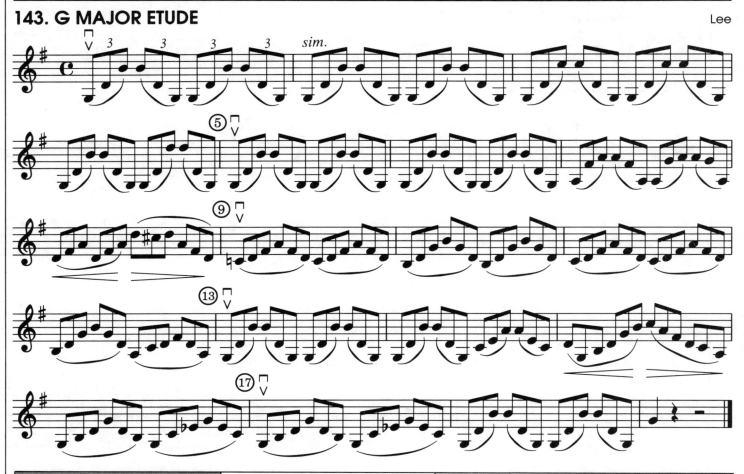

TREMOLO

Measured

Tremolo is played with rapid down and up bow movements on one note using an exact number of bow strokes.

144. F MAJOR ETUDE

Werner Op. 12

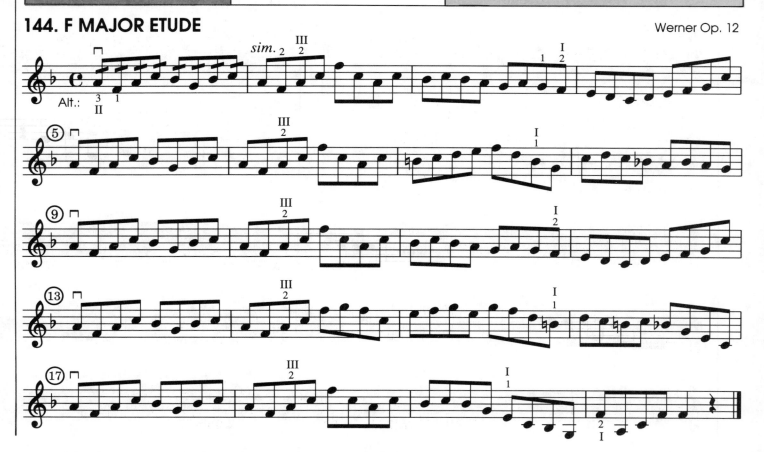

ETUDES

TREMOLO	 Unmeasured	Tremolo is played with rapid down and up bow movements on one note using an unmeasured number of bow strokes.

145. C MAJOR ETUDE

Dancla Op. 52

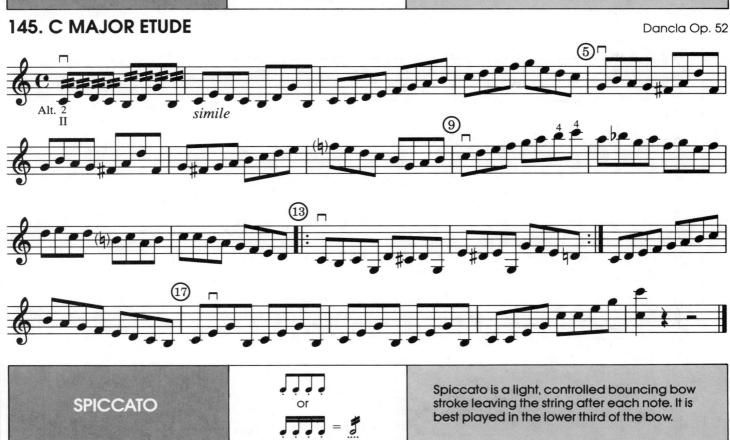

SPICCATO		Spiccato is a light, controlled bouncing bow stroke leaving the string after each note. It is best played in the lower third of the bow.

146. SPICCATO TRAINER

147. SPICCATO ETUDE

Kayser

MAJOR SCALES

MINOR SCALES (Melodic)

a minor

e minor

b minor

d minor

g minor

c minor

CHROMATIC SCALES

G CHROMATIC

C CHROMATIC

FINGER TWISTERS AND TECHNIC BUILDERS

INSTRUCTIONS

1. Play each measure at least four times with each assigned Rhythm or Bowing Pattern.
2. Start slowly, and upon mastering the exercise(s) gradually increase the tempo.
3. Use each key signature to establish a new finger pattern for each exercise.
4. Play each exercise (finger pattern) on all four strings.
5. Listen carefully and think through each finger pattern to help achieve accurate intonation.

1. FIRST (I) POSITION

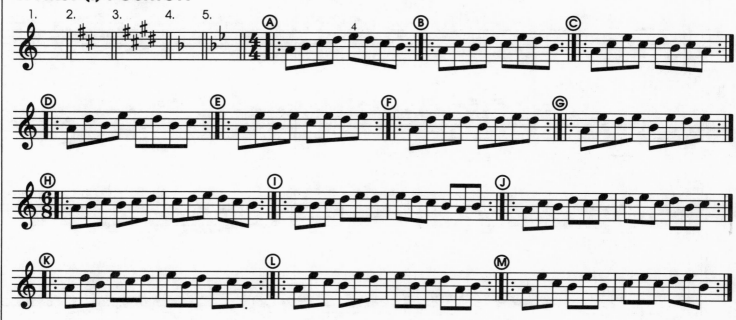

2. THIRD (III) POSITION

RHYTHM AND BOWING PATTERNS